GREEN
WITCHCRAFT

GREEN WITCHCRAFT

Magical ways to walk softly on the Earth

Marie Bruce

SIRIUS

SIRIUS

This edition published in 2022 by Sirius Publishing, a division of
Arcturus Publishing Limited,
26/27 Bickels Yard, 151–153 Bermondsey Street,
London SE1 3HA

All images courtesy of Shutterstock

ISBN: 978-1-3988-2585-7
AD010768UK

Printed in China

CONTENTS

Introduction..6

Chapter One: What is a Green Witch?...............................8

Chapter Two: The Green Witch's Pantry 18

Chapter Three: The Green Witch's Garden...................34

Chapter Four: Green Folklore 48

Chapter Five: Forest Witch..58

Chapter Six: The Language and Magic of Flowers.....70

Chapter Seven: The Poison Pathway...............................82

Chapter Eight: Green Witch Environmentalism..................94

Chapter Nine: Green Witch Activism

and Empowerment..106

Chapter Ten: Green Living and Giving 118

Afterword..126

INTRODUCTION
Follow the mossy stepping stones...

Do you ever feel a sense of enchantment as you wander around a woodland, or sink into the grass in a park or garden on a hot summer day, content to watch the clouds race and the trees sway? Have you ever stirred a simple cup of herbal tea with a wish in your heart and then imagined that wish coming true as you sipped the brew? Or perhaps you feel a strong affinity with birds and wildlife, convinced that they have a wise message for you? If so, it could be that you are a green witch.

The magic of the green witch has often been depicted in folklore, and she is a staple character in many fables. She is frequently shown living in a cottage at the edge of a dense forest, where she forages for food, remedies and supplies for the spells she casts over a bonfire in her tangled garden of herbs and flowers. She is sometimes old, sometimes young, usually living alone – or with sister witches – but she is always powerful. She lives in tune with the world around her, a student of the Earth, studying the lore of plants. She is both a guardian and protector of her environment, giving and receiving magical energy to work her will.

Such is the stereotype, yet the modern-day green witch is just as likely to be found living in a large city, foraging herbs from her windowsill or balcony, as she is to be living a rural life in the countryside. She might not be a woman at all, as more and more men are also finding the green path. Although I use the feminine pronoun throughout this book, it is of course a non-binary practice and green witchery is for everyone who is drawn to nature. It is for all those who find their soul stirred by the quickening of the Earth and who feel most at ease when they are in a green space, be that a garden, a park, a room full of houseplants or the dark forests we know from fairy tales.

Green witchcraft is a mossy labyrinth of stepping stones, designed to lead its practitioners right back into the ancient realm of forest lore, straight to the heart of Mother Earth, so tread lightly for she feels your presence. Step into this secret garden of magic and enchantment as you learn to see with glimmering green eyes.

Serene blessings,
Marie Bruce x

CHAPTER ONE
WHAT IS A GREEN WITCH?

As an Earth-based spirituality, witchcraft is intrinsically linked to nature and the environment. While all witches work with the Earth's power in some capacity, green witches dedicate their entire practice to the magic and lore of plants, trees, herbs and flowers. They immerse themselves in the natural world around them, taking great joy in the tiniest bud that pushes between the pavestones of a city street, or spending time with a favourite tree as if it were an old friend.

Green witches feel the life force of plants acutely, nurturing and caring for them like children, using them in spells, rituals and healing remedies. It is a much simpler practice than Wicca, which is high ceremonial magic. The green witch works predominantly alone from her own home and natural surroundings. Also known as a hedge witch, the green witch is a combination of environmentalist, activist, herbalist, healer, charmer and devotee to wildlife. So how do you know if you are a green witch? Look out for these signs.

Signs You Might Be a Green Witch

- You feel energized when out in nature.
- Green spaces make you feel happy and uplifted.
- You are inclined to grow plants and herbs.
- You enjoy gardening.
- Even in a small space, you bring nature in, introducing potted plants and crystals.
- You prefer the great outdoors and spend as much time outside as you can.
- You are intrigued by the many benefits of plants and their healing properties.
- You create "gardens" wherever you can – even on balconies, windowsills or in corridors.
- You feel an affinity with wildlife and chat to the birds, bees and wild creatures you meet.
- You feel saddened by environmental issues such as global warming.

If any of this seems familiar, then it is likely that you have a natural aptitude for green witchcraft. This book will help you to hone those skills into a positive practice.

Guardians of the Green

Those following the path of the green witch often see themselves as the guardians of the environment. They take their responsibility to the Earth very seriously and will campaign against the felling of healthy trees, deforestation, pollution, global warming and so on. At the same time, they are usually active in their communities, looking for ways to create or care for green spaces, clearing litter, raising awareness of local environmental issues and doing what they can to ensure that the world remains green and growing, healthy and abundant.

In this sense, green witches work on both a micro- and macro-cosmic scale. The microcosm is her own space, her home and garden. It is here that the bulk of her work is carried out, growing, harvesting and using herbs, casting spells and rituals and so on. Green witches tend to their own environment with all due diligence, ensuring they mitigate any negative impact on the planet. This might mean that they recycle, reuse and shop secondhand. It could also include a vegan or vegetarian diet, using natural cleaning products for housework and so on. Green witches try to live as ethically as possible, being mindful of the impact their daily habits and routines have on the environment.

At the same time, they will also work within the macrocosm of their immediate community and the world at large, supporting global issues such as sustainable energy, rewilding projects, equality, human and animal rights. In this way, green witches become activists, raising their voices to have a positive influence and impact on policies and politics, because when you feel a close connection to the Earth, you want to protect and defend it. In recent years, as we come to see the devastating effects of global warming, this kind of activism has become more ingrained into the practice of green witchery.

Notable Green Witches

Some green witches have been very outspoken about their wish to protect the planet, carrying the ideology of green witchcraft into the mainstream by publishing books, appearing on television, offering workshops and being key speakers at events and seminars. Here are a few of the most notable green witches of today.

STARHAWK When US feminist, Starhawk, first published her book *The Spiral Dance* in 1979, she could not possibly have known what she was starting, but it became one of the main inspirations behind the Goddess Movement in the 1970s, which has proved a popular path for many pagans to follow. Starhawk has been very vocal about her belief that the Earth is a living being – one which we all have a duty to care for and protect. Discover more at starhawk.org.

GLENNIE KINDRED As a British artist and writer, Glennie Kindred has a reputation for exploring sacred meaning in her native landscape and looking at her place within it. She brings her love of nature to the page, writing and illustrating her beautiful books, which are full of herb lore, sacred sites and self-empowerment achieved via a spiritual connection with the Earth. She gives talks and workshops to help people reconnect with the environment in a spiritual way. Find her at glenniekindred.co.uk.

EMMA RESTALL ORR A British Druid, Emma Restall Orr has walked the pagan path for many years. She is a well-known figure in the community, frequently appearing at Witchfest festival and at sacred sites such as Stonehenge. She has written several books on her green practice, including introductions for beginners, as well as memoirs of her life as a Druid Priestess. In writing such books, she has effectively documented Druidry, which is more commonly seen as an oral tradition, thus helping those who seek a greener path to find their way more easily.

The Witch Wound

In the past, both witches and Druids were persecuted for their beliefs and they were often executed. In England and the US, witches were hanged; in Europe they were burned at the stake, while in Scotland they were either burned at the stake or in a barrel. Interestingly, Wales didn't succumb to the witch craze and only a handful of so-called witches were ever executed there. What did the Welsh see that the rest of Britain, Europe and the US failed to register?

It is also interesting that many of the *accusers* were also women: neighbours, former friends, love rivals – and sometimes even relatives of the accused. It is thought these women were often acting from spite or envy, bearing a grudge and pointing the finger to exact revenge for a perceived slight or wrongdoing. After all, what better way to get rid of your husband's lover than by accusing her of witchcraft? Women turning against women – a phenomenon called female relational aggression – was, along with social cleansing, one of the driving forces behind the witch trials.

The witch craze lasted from the 14th to the 18th century and many lives were lost because of it. This historical or hereditary trauma, known as the Witch Wound, is still occasionally felt by modern witches. It is experienced as a feeling of uneasiness when faced with certain places or types of magic. It can even lead to a reluctance to experience any degree of power at all, both personally and professionally. It is especially likely to be felt when visiting a place, such as a castle dungeon or known execution site, where witches were held, tortured or killed. Famous examples of these are Lancaster Castle, where the Pendle Witches were held prior to execution in 1612, or the Witch's Stone in Dornoch, Scotland, which marks the spot where Janet Horne, the last person to be tried and executed for witchcraft in Britain, was burned to death in 1727.

In recent times, there have been attempts to heal this ancient wound, by honouring the lives of those accused. On March 8, 2022, International Women's Day, the Scottish first minster Nicola Sturgeon offered a formal apology to all those accused and executed in Scotland between the 16th and 18th centuries. Hopefully, other countries will soon follow suit.

THE
WITCHES
OF
NORTHAMPTON-
SHIRE.

Agnes Browne. } *Arthur Bill.*
Ioane Vaughan. } *Hellen Ienkenson* } Witches.
Mary Barber.

Who were all executed at *Northampton* the 22. of
Iuly last. 1 6 1 2.

LONDON,
Printed by *Tho: Purfoot*, for *Arthur*
Iohnson. 1 6 1 2.

A Green Witch's Tools and Attire

Before you begin your foray into the realms of green witchcraft, it is a good idea to try and collect the following tools, which will help you in your rituals and protect you as you ramble through the countryside. You don't need to spend a lot of money or gather them all at once. As you will see, many of these tools are common household items, others can be handmade or found in thrift shops.

- Wellies or boots to keep your feet dry when trudging through muddy forests.
- A basket for foraged items or to carry materials for rituals.
- A green witch cloak to offer warmth and camouflage, encouraging wildlife to come closer and befriend you.

- Botanical books/apps for checking and double-checking species and identifications.

- Notebooks to record your travels, spells and rituals, and to profile herbs.

- Secateurs, a small scythe or bolline (ritual knife) to harvest herbs, berries and blossom.

- A mortar and pestle to grind dried herbs for spells.

- A cauldron for burning fire spells, or to hold water for divination.

- Gardening gloves to protect your hands from thorny plants that like to bite back!

- An altar pentacle to charge your herbs and crystals with magical energy.

- A chalice for ritual wine and home-made potions.

- Consumables – everything you need to make your magic fly! Spell jars, pouches, string, candles, crystals, essential oils and so on.

- A green space – this could be a garden, balcony, local park or woodland.

- PLANTS – the very essence of green witchcraft. You won't get very far without their help!

And on we continue to the next mossy stepping stone...

CHAPTER TWO
THE GREEN WITCH'S PANTRY

S tep into the green witch's pantry and you will find a
plethora of herbs and flowers, all lined up in jars on
a shelf, drying on racks and strewn across doorways
and windowsills for various spells and rituals. In the past,
such pantries were known as still rooms, in which the lady
of the manor, or the chatelaine, would concoct remedies,
soaps, candles, cordials and tisanes, for the good of all those
who lived beneath her roof. It was an important job and one
which the chatelaine would have learned from her mother and
grandmother as a child, in preparation for her future marriage.
It could also be a dangerous task – especially during the rise of
the witch craze, as any mistakes could lead to accusations of
witchcraft or poisoning.

The 16th-century Queen of France, Catherine de Medici, was well known for dabbling in herbs, potions and lethal poisons, as well as spellcraft. One can only imagine the things that might have been conjured in *her* still room, which was purported to have hundreds of secret compartments hidden in the panelled walls, thought to house her collection

of poisons. You wouldn't want to take tea with her! The modern witch's pantry is much more mundane and it needn't be a room at all. Your witch's pantry could be a cupboard in the kitchen, a dresser, a bookcase, a wooden chest or a set of shelves. Whatever you choose will be determined by your space and budget, but it is here that you will keep your jars of dried herbs and spices, essential oils, spell jars, pouches and candles, incense, smudge bundles and crystals. Pick whatever space appeals to you, or whatever you have to hand. There is no need to buy a new item of furniture – you could perhaps simply clear out a drawer and use that as your witch's pantry. Keep your tools, such as your pentacle, mortar and pestle and so on, close by so that you have everything to hand when you need it.

Mother Earth

Green witchcraft is part of the pagan path, which means that all green witches believe that the planet is a sacred entity in its own right. We see the Earth as our mother, for we could not survive without her nurturing, nourishing and abundant provision. We live off her generosity in the crops that we eat and the food that we grow. Most green witches believe in sustainable and responsible farming, turning away from produce that has been flown across the world and choosing to buy locally grown produce instead or to grow what they can themselves.

Honoured as an aspect of the divine feminine, our planet is frequently known as Mother Earth, Gaia or Mother Nature. Green witches are her protectors and collaborators, working with the cycles of the moon and the seasons to nurture their own green spaces. Green witches believe that pollution, consumerism and deforestation are having a negative impact and that we are biting the hand that feeds us. Without caring for the Earth by living sustainably, our planet cannot continue to sustain and care for us indefinitely, so our daily habits need to become eco-friendlier, if we are to reverse the damage that has already been done.

Herbalism

Growing, tending, drying and using herbs in spellcraft is the main business of the green witch. She grows her own ingredients for spells as much as possible, forages for what she can, shares and trades supplies with like-minded friends and generally gets her hands dirty! She is never happier than when rambling through the woods hunting for mushrooms, or knee-deep in the garden transplanting seedlings into beds and tucking them in with care. She loves the scent of the earth, the feel of the soil between her fingertips, the softness of new shoots and leaves coming up. Her soul runs as green as vegetation after a spring shower and she is in her element cultivating herbs, plants, flowers and trees.

In its purest form, green witchery involves growing things, but if you don't have particularly green fingers, you can forage from a friend's garden or use dried herbs from the supermarket if needs be. If you want to be authentic to the green witch's way, however, you should really grow your own plants – even just a couple of pots on a windowsill.

We will be looking at how to create both indoor and outdoor gardens in the next chapter. For now, it's worth noting that getting acquainted with fresh herbs, flowers and plants is a key part of life for most green witches. While a comprehensive list of herbs is somewhat beyond the scope of this little book, here are a few of the most magical herbs and plants used by witches.

- **Angelica** – Also known as Masterwort, angelica is a good plant for protection rituals and can help ward away evil energies.

- **Aloe** – Great for treating minor burns, heat rash and skin irritations, aloe can also be used in beauty potions and to treat the complexion.

- **Basil** – A good power booster for spells, basil is great for protection magic.

- **Bay** – The prosperity herb! Growing bay is said to bring wealth and good fortune. Plant it near your front door to bring prosperity to your home.

- **Broom** – A magical shrub that has been used to make brooms or besoms for centuries. Great for cleansing rituals and the protection of boundaries.

- **Burdock** – Thought to guard against negative energies, ill-wishing and bad vibes, burdock has purification and protective properties.

- **Chamomile** – A herb of rest, relaxation, anti-stress and soothing sleep. Great for night-time teas, healing tisanes and moments of peaceful meditation.

- **Catnip** – This little herb famously sends cats nuts! They love it because it gives them a natural feeling of euphoria. A great one to grow if you have feline familiars.

- **Cinnamon** – Ground cinnamon is commonly added to prosperity and abundance spells. Add it to teas for a warming and soothing effect.

- **Clover** – A magical little plant said to bring good luck, clover is often used in spells to reverse a period of bad fortune or to bring about a lucky break of some kind.

 **Clove** – Clove is used to stop gossip, slander, sabotage and back-stabbing. It is also a well-known cure for toothache.

 **Dandelion** – Much maligned as a common weed, the humble dandelion can be used in spells for transformation, ambition and recognition. Steeped as a tea, it is a great aid to the digestive system.

 **Elder** – Both the fruit and the flowers of the elder tree are beneficial and can be used in cooking and when brewing cordials and wines. In spellcraft, elder is used to define and protect boundaries and also to connect with the Crone Goddess or Elder Mother (see Chapter Four).

 **Eucalyptus** – Great for steam baths to ease congestion and can also be dried and burned to clear obstacles from your path. Good to add to smudge bundles.

 **Fennel** – Fennel seeds can be added to spell pouches for protection and purification. The plant can also be hung over thresholds to protect boundaries.

 **Fern** – Symbolizing the slow unfolding of events, ferns are said to represent love, protection and patience.

- **Geranium** – A pretty plant that signifies love, especially self-love. Geranium tea is very good for easing menstrual cramps and tensions.

- **Gorse** – A prickly shrub that can bloom with golden flowers throughout the year. Best planted by garden gates, paths and doors to ward away unwelcome visitors.

- **Hyssop** – A lovely plant that attracts all kinds of wildlife, from birds and bees to butterflies and moths. Hyssop is a staple in the cottage garden and great in borders. Magically it can be used to attune with the fey, the Earth and wildlife.

- **Hawthorn** – May blossom is said to hold the spirit of the spring goddess and so hawthorn – also known as the May tree – is honoured on May Day. Traditionally it is one of the fairy triad trees of oak, ash and thorn. It's said where these three grow together, fairy activity is present.

- **Holly** – Represents the Green Man in his aspect as Holly King, the ruler of the dark season. Holly is great for protection and is traditionally viewed as the Yule plant.

Ivy – Magically, ivy can be used in binding spells, to prevent someone from acting against you or to keep secrets. It also represents the Green Woman or Wode Wives (see Chapter Four).

Jasmine – An ingredient in bath potions and beauty treatments, jasmine is thought to bring love to one who wears it.

Juniper – Offering protection from unforeseen events and accidents, juniper is also said to attract love and positive attention. If placed by the door, it will guard against thieves and intruders.

Lavender – A fantastic all-rounder, lavender is good for all kinds of magic, predominantly love, protection, purification, healing and sleep. If you grow nothing else, cultivate some lavender!

Mint – Powerful herb for prosperity, abundance, wealth, money, savings, ambition and career progression. Also known for its uplifting and refreshing properties.

Mugwort – A traditional witch's herb, mugwort is often used to reduce swelling, bruising and to treat mild tummy upsets. In magic, it is regarded as one of the wise woman's herbs as it was used to bring on visions, prophetic dreams and clairvoyance. It was often given to women to induce menstruation.

Nettle – Most frequently used in magic to stop gossip and spite, nettles can be added to spells to make someone feel the sting of their own words.

Patchouli – A great herb for prosperity, protection, love, passion and romance, so why wouldn't you want some patchouli in your life?

Rowan – The berries and bark are used in protection charms and spells.

Sage – The purification herb, sage is frequently made into bundles and burned in ritual cleansings. These bundles are called smudge sticks and you can easily make them yourself at home (see page 32). It is good for healing, particularly healing a rift between two parties. It can also be added to protection and prosperity magic.

Thyme – Another herb that is said to aid in psychic visions, divinations and prophecy.

Valerian – A great aid to restful sleep or to bring about dreams of a future lover.

- 🌿 **Vervain** – A good protection herb, particularly useful when danger is ever-present, so for the safeguarding of members of the armed forces and emergency services, for example.

- 🌿 **Wormwood** – Also known as the Green Fairy, wormwood is said to bring about visions, inspiration and a feeling of euphoria. When steeped in alcohol, it becomes "the poet's draught", or absinthe, beloved of the Romantic poets such as Lord Byron and Percy Bysshe Shelley. These days it is more commonly sold as Pernod.

- 🌿 **Yarrow** – Yarrow can be used to break a fever, bring down a temperature and ease digestive complaints. When drunk as a tea, it can help to boost immunity and ward off seasonal colds and flu, plus it is said to be a good cure for a hangover.

These are just some of the plants used by witches in their magic and this list is by no means exhaustive. Feel free to research the herbs, plants and flowers that are native to your own area and their magical and medicinal uses. Be sure to use a good botanical encyclopaedia when trying to identify plants in the wild and remember, there are no such things as *weeds*, there are only *wild flowers*.

How to Make a Herb-Drying Rack

Items required: Five twigs or sticks, a ball of twine, metal shower curtain hooks, coloured ribbon (optional).

Are you ready to start foraging for magical items? If so, go out into the forest, your garden or a local park on a windy day. Find a place with many trees and stand beneath them. Close your eyes and silently ask the tree spirits to guide you to the best naturally shed twigs. Gather five twigs, each about 30cm in length and 2–5cm thick. Take them home, giving thanks to the trees and dry out the twigs thoroughly.

Once dry, lay the twigs in the shape of a pentacle or five-pointed star and secure each point with string. Add equal lengths of string or pretty ribbon from both ends of the star so that you can hang it in a horizontal position, to create a rack. Next, on the branches of the pentacle, attach the shower curtain hooks, from which you can hang bunches of herbs and flowers upside down to dry. Finally, find a space in your home to hang the drying rack – traditionally this would be the kitchen, still room or conservatory.

Sage and Lavender Smudge Bundles

Items required: Enough fresh sage and lavender to create a couple of bundles, natural twine or string.

Harvest enough fresh stems of sage and lavender to make two smudge bundles, each approximately 5cm in diameter. Begin with the sage, making a small posy in your hand, adding a stem at a time, then adding stems of lavender on top. Make sure the bundle is as even as possible, then holding it firmly, begin to wrap the string around it, moving from the stems of the herbs to the top and back again so the string criss-crosses and secures the herbs in place.

Tie the string tightly to secure the bundle and hang it upside down from your drying rack. Leave in place until all the herbs have dried thoroughly, right the way through. To use, light the end of the smudge bundle until it glows red, then blow out the flame and allow the bundle to smoulder. Gently waft the fragrant smoke around yourself, your home and property, to cleanse the area of all negative energy and bad vibes. When you have finished, stub out the bundle and leave it in an ashtray until you are sure it has been extinguished. Repeat each month as the moon wanes to keep your space positive and peaceful.

CHAPTER THREE
THE GREEN WITCH'S GARDEN

Green witchery is all about communing with the Earth, getting outside and enjoying the greenery that gives the practice its name. It is essential that you have a green space or garden of your own, but don't worry if you don't have one outside, as you can create an indoor garden, which is just as magical. Attuning with plants and trees is good for the soul. It decreases stress levels and lowers blood pressure – and plants naturally help with pollution by purifying the air around them, so there are many benefits to nurturing a garden of your own.

The Nemeton Grove

In Celtic and Druidic culture, the nemeton grove was a sacred outdoor space where special gatherings, rituals and celebrations would be held. It was similar to an outdoor church – a place for rituals and important decisions made for the good of the whole clan. The green witch's garden is her own nemeton grove, for she tends to it as the sacred space it is. It is here that the green witch grows ingredients for spells and potions, where she studies herbs and their properties and where she interacts with the wildlife, actively encouraging birds, bees, foxes and hares to visit her garden. The witch's nemeton grove is likely to have a special seating area, perhaps a table for potting seedlings or writing herb profiles in notebooks, a water feature of some kind – be this a simple bird bath or an elaborate pond – and lots of feeders and habitats so wildlife can thrive. The witch's garden is always a hive of activity, even in winter as birds come to rely on the food she provides.

Creating an Outdoor Garden

If you have an outdoor space, you can create a beautiful witch's garden and nemeton grove of your own. Designing and nurturing a garden is a long-term commitment, but it is something that brings joy to many people. Think beyond regimental rows of flower beds and try to craft something that has wildness at its heart. Your garden should reflect your interests in green witchery – it doesn't matter if your neighbours don't approve of you ripping out a brick barbecue so you can build a medicinal herb garden. It is your space to use as you wish, so plant herbs, flowers, shrubs and trees to your heart's content.

Take inspiration from the cloister gardens of old convents and monasteries, if you want to see what a useful magical garden looks like. Visit stately homes for inspiration and recreate your favourite aspects of their grounds on a smaller scale. Try to create a garden that appeals to all of your senses, so plant flowers for colour and fragrance, add different levels and different-sized shrubs to appeal to the eye, include both evergreen and variegated foliage, plant herbs for flavour and texture and add chimes and feeders to fill the space with sound.

Make the space as magical as you can, but don't forget to leave a little corner of your garden quite wild in order to encourage the fey folk! Remember that any garden takes time to mature and grow, so you are not going to have a witch's garden overnight, but you can begin with whatever you have, be that potted herbs from the supermarket, or cuttings from your neighbours. Make a start and enjoy the process, because there is nothing more charming than picking chamomile flowers from your own garden to brew into a soothing cup of tea.

Creating an Indoor Garden

What if you don't have an outside space of your own? Can you still be a green witch if you don't even have a balcony? Of course you can! There are many plants that thrive indoors so houseplants are your best friends. In fact, most green witches don't confine their foliage just to outside, they tend to have indoor spaces full of greenery too. Cacti, miniature rose trees, crocuses, ferns, basil, lemon balm and mint all do well in pots, so visit the local garden centre and see what appeals to you in their houseplant section.

All the same rules apply for an indoor garden as for the outdoor one, so create a collection of potted plants in your home that stimulates all the senses. Have flowering plants for colour, herbs on the windowsill for flavour, use hanging baskets, plant stands and shelving to create different levels of greenery. You can even add a bird feeder and a suction bath to the outside of a window to encourage your feathered friends to come along for dinner and a splash around, so that you can enjoy the melody of their frolicking and singing. Nestle crystals in among the foliage for added sparkle and hang a Green Man plaque on the wall to honour the spirit of the greenwood. Surround yourself with the nature that you love and, even if you live in a high-rise apartment, you will soon feel that you have an enchanted garden of your own that you can't wait to come home to, living your best green witch life.

Gardening by the Moon

Witches observe the cycles of the moon, and our magic is cast in accordance with the lunar cycle. Green witchery is no different. Just as the moon has a gravitational pull on the tides of the ocean, it also has an affect the growth of plants. With this in mind, most green witches tend to garden in accordance with the phases of the moon, as follows.

- **Dark Moon** – This is traditionally a time of rest, just before the new moon appears in the sky, so it's the best time to read gardening magazines and books on green witchcraft, to catalogue seeds and so on.

- **New Moon** – Great for making plans, designing flower beds and plotting garden improvements on paper, or collecting seeds ready for planting. Also a good time to plant leafy plants such as ferns, shrubs and trees.

- **Waxing Moon** – As the moon grows from new to full, this is the time to plant new seeds, put your garden plans into action and move seedlings outdoors. Great for planting anything that bears berries or fruit.

- **Full Moon** – The best time to repot anything that needs more space, to move plants from one area of the garden to another, to harvest fruit, berries and herbs or to cut flowers for the house.

Waning Moon – As the moon wanes and the light diminishes, now is a good time to tend to the soil, to feed the roots and offer libations (traditionally called wassailing) or to plant root crops, such as carrots and parsnips. This is also a good time to plant a new crop of bulbs that you would like to flourish the following year, so bluebells, daffodils and so on. Deadheading, pruning and tree lopping should also be done during a waning moon.

In addition to following the lunar cycle, green witches also work in accordance with theseasons in general when it comes to maintaining their gardens.

- **Spring** – Sow seeds and young plants, move seedlings outdoors.
- **Summer** – Feed plants and cultivate beds, do your weeding, maintain lawns and hedgerows.
- **Autumn** – Harvest, clear leaves, bring vulnerable plants indoors, prepare for winter by strengthening boundaries and fences.
- **Winter** – Feed wildlife, de-ice ponds and water features, lop and prune.

Invoke a Guardian for your Garden

Items required: A garden lantern and candle or tealight, a fairy sun-catcher.
Moon phase: Full moon.

Once you have created your garden, you might like to invoke a guardian to watch over it. Witches see the lifeforce in everything, which means that each plant has its own spirit. Overall, the fey or faerie folk are said to be the guardians of the natural world, including gardens, parks and woodlands. You can invoke a fey guardian for your space in the following way. To begin with, light a tealight and place it in a lantern that is suitable for outdoors and carry it to your garden, along with the sun-catcher. Place them both on the floor or a table and breathe deeply three times. Close your eyes and say:

Guardian of this space, fey spirit of my dreaming

I ask that you protect this place, this realm of growth and greening

Help me to create a sacred grove of peace

A spiritual retreat beneath enchanted trees

Guard and guide me as I tend our garden with care

Impart your shining wisdom in this place and leave it there

So mote it be.

Find a place to keep the lantern and hang the sun-catcher where it will bounce the light around the garden. Spend as much time in your nemeton grove as you can and enjoy the space you have conjured.

CHAPTER FOUR
GREEN FOLKLORE

D o you know what to do if you are being pixie-led, or what time of year is the most auspicious for asking the Green Man for a boon? Green witchcraft is naturally steeped in fey folklore, because you are working with the forest and plants, which the fey spirits protect. Many green witches like to work faerie craft too, communing with the nature spirits of flowers, trees and hedgerows as they forage and work their rituals. In this chapter you will learn more about these enchanted beings.

The Green Man and Woodwose

The Green Man is the spirit of foliage and trees. Made of leaves and bark, root and branch, he is present in every shrub, plant and tree. Also known as a Woodwose, he is the guardian of the forest, sometimes referred to as the Lord of the Wildwood. Look closely and you will see his face in the bark. Glance up and you are likely to see him carved into the vaults of churches, or spouting rainwater from above in castles, old universities and other buildings. He was a popular motif of medieval architecture, so it is highly likely that he has been watching over you from one vantage point or another at some stage in your life. His presence in churches signifies the transition from the old pagan ways to the new Christian religion, as the stonemasons would incorporate his face in an act of reverence for the Old Religion, as paganism is sometimes known.

Whenever you are in a woodland or forest, or even in the smallest copse of trees and shrubs, the Green Man is present. He changes with the seasons, his foliage face going from spring green to autumn gold to frosted bark, as the Wheel of the Year turns, but he is ever-present. You might sense him, watching you from behind the leaves. It can be quite a spooky feeling at times, but he is simply guarding his territory, as any good sentry would do. Look out for him next time you are in a wooded area, an old church or university. See if you can see him peering at you from the bark or the stone foliage. Like the Great Goddess, the Green Man has several aspects and he is known by different names.

Aspects of the Green Man

- **Holly King –** The Green Man of the dark half of the year, coming into power on the autumnal equinox. He presides over the winter months in the forest.

- **Oak King –** Brother to the Holly King, the Oak King presides over the lighter half of the year. He does battle with his brother on the spring equinox and wins, bringing in the spring and summer months. He presides over the forest until the next battle in autumn, when the Holly King triumphs and takes over once again.

- **John Barleycorn –** The spirit of the harvest, John Barleycorn is the sacrificial god of the crops, laying down his life before the scythe in order to feed the population.

- **Herne the Hunter –** Another Lord of the Trees and the Hunt, Herne is closely associated with Windsor Great Park, where he stepped in front of a rampaging stag to protect King Richard II of England. His name has become intertwined with Green Man mythology and folklore. He is viewed as an aspect of the witch's god, along with his older Celtic counterpart, Cernunnos.

- **Jack in the Green/Puck/Robin Hood –** In this aspect, the Green Man becomes the trickster, playing jokes on travellers, leading them astray, or exacting a price for passing through his realm. This could be a piece of jewellery or a coin, or it could be a blood price, in the form of cuts and scratches from thorny plants.

- **Jack Frost –** the Green Man of the winter woods and counterpart to Jack in the Green. As his name suggests, Jack Frost paints the trees with frost and snow, hangs icicles from the branches and turns the forest into a winter wonderland of silver and white.

Ritual to Ask the Green Man for a Boon

Items required: A pretty crystal for an offering.
Moon phase: Full moon.

Magical tradition states that, twice a year, you may ask the Green Man for a magical boon. This request should take place at either the summer or winter solstice, when the respective Oak and Holly Kings are at the height of their power. If you want something to come to you, then beseech the Oak King. If you want to remove something, such as illness, then ask the Holly King to take it away with him when he falls. You can also request seasonal boons, such as a lovely summer holiday from the Oak King or a fantastic Yuletide from the Holly King.

The timing of your ritual will depend on what it is you require and which aspect of the Green Man you are invoking, but it should always be cast on the full moon, preferably outdoors under the trees. Take your crystal with you and find a tree that feels friendly and comfortable with your presence. Introduce yourself and state your purpose and intention, asking for the boon you require, then say:

I have a wish that I wish to be seen
I bring it here to the Man in the Green
Oak/Holly King, grant me this boon
And let my request be granted right soon
In love and trust I make this plea
And leave below this gift for thee.

Place the crystal at the root of the tree and leave it there. Your wish should be granted before your chosen Green King's demise, so within three months.

Faces in the Bark Ritual

Items required: A large sheet of paper, charcoal or wax crayons.
Moon phase: Perform anytime.

Take your art supplies with you to the forest or park and look for faces in the bark. Once you find the Green Man looking back at you, take a bark rubbing of his image and bring it home with you. You can then frame it and use it to decorate your altar or sacred space.

The Green Woman and Wode Wives

The female counterpart to the Green Man is the Green Woman, also known as a Wode Wife. She is the fey creature who connects the masculine energy of the forest with the ancient feminine energy of Mother Earth. Although she is less common in folklore and architecture than the Green Man, she is also ever-present in the woods and her energies are usually more gentle and much less spooky.

In folklore, the Wode Wife is a skilled herbalist and healer, a green witch, who can appear as a female form made of moss and bark, foliage and blossom, although in some legends she takes on human form and appears with long blonde hair, wearing a white dress. In this respect, J R R Tolkien's character, Galadriel, Queen of the Elves in *The Lord of the Rings* trilogy, is a depiction of a Wode Wife. As with many of the female fey spirits, Wode Wives are said to have very long hair, dressed in leaves, berries and blossom. They are believed to appreciate offerings of bread and honey.

Aspects of the Green Woman

- **Dryads** – In Greek mythology, the dryads were the female spirits of trees. They could leave their tree for short periods, but must always return. If the tree was cut down in their absence, they would wander as lost spirits without a home. If the tree was cut down while the dryad spirit was within, she too would die.

- **May Queen** – The spirit of the spring goddess, embodied in the white blossom of the hawthorn tree, which flowers each May. To bring May blossom indoors is bad luck, and you should only cut hawthorn blossom on May's Eve or May Day.

- **Maid Marian** – The counterpart to Robin Hood, Maid Marian is the matriarch of his band of Merry Men. Like many Wode Wives, she tends to wounds using the healing power of herbs, and can vanish into the forest without trace.

- **Elder Mother** – The Crone spirit of the elder tree, the Elder Mother is the wise woman of the forest. It is considered very bad luck to cut or prune an elder tree without the Elder Mother's permission. Burning elder wood was said to bring a year and a day of misfortune, so respect the Elder!

Have You Been Pixie-Led?

Taking a walk or ride in among the trees can be a risky business and it can by easy to lose your way. If you find yourself lost in the woods, having gone round and round in circles, it could be that you have been pixie-led – that is, the forest spirits have been leading you astray! This is something that the trickster aspects of the Green Man, such as Puck or Robin Hood, and the Wode Wives are thought to do. They use the sounds of the forest, such as falling trees and branches to confuse you and lead you a merry dance. So, if you keep hearing the snap of a twig behind you, but no one is there, it could be that the green spirits of the forest are playing games with you. According to tradition, the best way to end their game is to turn and wear your coat inside-out to show that you have nothing to hide. That way, you will be led safely back out of the woods.

CHAPTER FIVE
FOREST WITCH

During medieval times, much of the UK was covered in woodland, which stretched from the south of England right up to the Caledonian Forest in Scotland. It was called the Medieval Forest, sometimes the Kingswood, and it was a hive of activity from royal hunting parties chasing deer to cut-throats and outlaws lying in wait for unwary travellers.

In some areas, small pockets of this forest still remain. One clear indicator of an ancient forest is the presence of English bluebells, so if you live in the UK and you have a small bluebell wood near you, the chances are it was once a part of the Medieval Forest. This forest was introduced and ring-fenced by the Normans for their hunting activities, causing much social unrest among the less fortunate, who were forbidden to forage, snare or hunt there. To do so was known as "trespassing against the vert and the venison" which could lead to serious punishment. There are still laws in many woodlands that forbid removing items or picking flowers, so check before you go foraging.

Many green witches feel a special affinity with the forest and enjoy spending time there. There is a deep natural magic in any woodland. In all seasons, forests are enchanting places to visit. From the first stirrings of life in spring, to the green-tinged light that fills a summer woodland; from the russet, bronze and gold of autumn leaves to the shimmering frosted evergreens and bare branches of winter, the woodland is always a place of vibrant colour and texture.

A forest is a place of magic and fairy tale, of spooky shadows and strange sounds. It can be easy to feel unnerved when lost and alone in the woods. Soldiers call this "jungle fear," and learning how to control it is part of military training. This fear stems, in part, from the separation we now have from the natural world around us. No longer living closely to the rhythm of the land, it can be very easy for a modern city-dweller to feel uneasy in the midst of a forest, but there isn't really anything to be afraid of. The trees can't hurt you and most wildlife will be inclined to avoid you, rather than attack you. That said, there can be something rather fun about being unsettled in this way and lots of woodland trusts hold spooky events in the forest during autumn, so check what is happening in your local woods if that's something that appeals. Sherwood Forest holds such ghostly occasions every October, which are great fun. Whichever forest you visit, always be sure to abide by the local rules of that woodland and the Countryside Code.

The Lungs of the Earth

Forests are a vital part of the natural world and we need them now more than ever. As trees take in carbon dioxide and expel oxygen, they are great air purifiers and can help to combat pollution and global warming. Younger trees take on more carbon dioxide than older ones, which is the logic behind cutting down mature trees and replacing them with saplings. This is thought to help reduce pollution, especially in cities. However, if this continues indefinitely, it means that future generations will not know the thrill of visiting a centuries-old tree, such as the Major Oak in Sherwood Forest, so we also need to protect our mature trees as well.

Shared Breathing with Trees

Items required: A friendly tree.
Moon phase: Perform during a waxing to full moon.

Because humans and trees each need what the other expels, shared breathing is a great ritual to perform in a woodland. Go to a place where you can stand or sit comfortably beneath a tree. If you have trees in your garden that is great, but you can also visit a park or forest. Get comfortable under the boughs of the tree. Lean against the trunk if you can and tilt your head back to gaze up at the branches stretching out above you.

Close your eyes and begin some ritual breathing. Breathe in deeply through your nose for a count of four seconds, hold your breath for four seconds, then breathe out for another four seconds. As you do this, visualize your outward breath and carbon dioxide feeding the tree above you, while your inward breath takes in the oxygen that the tree has expelled. Continue sharing breath with the tree in this way for as long as you feel comfortable. The good thing about this exercise is that no one else knows what you are doing. To anyone who passes by, you are simply sitting beneath a tree in a relaxed and meditative state.

Earth Light

On occasion, if the conditions are right, you might be lucky enough to witness the phenomenon of earth light, or living light. This is when a tree or shrub appears to glow in a green and golden light. The shimmering effect all around the tree looks like a magical portal to another realm, but, in fact, it is the scientific process known as bioluminescence. There are differing opinions on what causes it but one possible explanation is that it occurs when sunlight hits the chlorophyll that gives plants their green colour. I have witnessed earth light once myself, when I was a young girl, and it was an extremely magical experience. It is a beautiful natural phenomenon, similar to the Northern Lights, and something you will never forget if you are lucky enough to witness it. Traditionally, earth light was thought to be a portal into the fairy realms and so if you see it, you should make a wish.

The Fairy Triad

Another portal to the fairy realm was the fairy triad, made up of oak, ash and thorn trees. Where these three trees grow together, it is said to be a sacred grove where fairy activity is said to be strongest. In folklore, it was said that people would be kidnapped by the fey if they walked through the fairy triad, only to return decades later, much older and raving about fairyland.

The fairy triad was also said to be a good place to meet a fairy lover, a Wode Wife or to make a wish, especially if you went there at the fairy hours of dawn or dusk. However, you should never leave a baby or child there unattended or the fey might replace them with a changeling. Oak, ash and thorn are all trees that the Druids revered, so they were viewed with disdain by the early Christians, which could explain some of these superstitions.

Foraging

The forest is full of treasure – and foraging is about using the gifts of nature in your magic. It is a fun activity, but foraging should always be conducted with respect. Never take more than you need and ask permission from the spirit of the plant or tree first. Some woodlands have strict rules about foraging and many wild flowers are protected, including bluebells, so you should not pick them. Remember that some woodlands are also privately owned and while the landowners allow the public access, these green spaces should not be foraged without permission from the estate manager.

It goes without saying that you should never dig up plants or remove bulbs from the ground, nor should you scrape lichen from the trees. In general, only forage what the wood no longer needs, such as twigs and leaves from the forest floor. If you are picking berries, make sure you can identify them correctly so you don't make dangerous mistakes: lethal hemlock can be confused for harmless elder, which is often used in cooking! So be careful and use your

common sense. If you don't know what it is, leave it be. Remember that some plants are toxic when touched and even the humble rose carries poison on its thorns, so wear gloves or carry antiseptic cream with you. Below are just a few suggestions as to what you might forage and use in your green witchcraft.

- Fallen leaves, especially in autumn. These make great botanical displays in a Book of Shadows or hung in frames. (The Book of Shadows is a witch's collection of spells, charms, rituals and so on – sort of like a magical diary.)

- Pinecones, acorns and seed pods are good for all aspects of abundance magic and prosperity spells. They can also be used in fertility magic too.

- Dead branches can be repurposed as magical wands, staffs and broom handles.

- Fallen twigs can be fashioned into all kinds of altar and wall decorations, from pentagrams to crescent moons.

- Pine needles can be added to home-made incense and burned on charcoal blocks for prosperity and winter magic.

- Soil from the forest floor is a great way to connect with a distant sacred place when you are back home, so take a small spell jar and fill it with earth from Sherwood, Epping or the Caledonian Forest – or your own local sacred woodland. Only take a small amount of topsoil away with you. You can add a pinch of this to boundary spells and grounding magic.

- Berries make good natural dyes for magical craft projects and, of course, some, such as blackberries, are edible and are tasty in pies and cordials.

- Blossoms such as elderflower make good bath potions and cordials, as well as natural dyes.

- Mushrooms and fungi – be very careful with these. Many are toxic so these are perhaps safest left alone, though you can always take photos or make sketches for your Book of Shadows.

- Nuts are good for abundance spells and, of course, there is great joy in hunting for chestnuts to roast in autumn, or conkers for games with the kids.

Other Forest Witch Tips

There are many ways you can incorporate the woods into your magical practice and if you are lucky enough to live close to a forest or park then you should make the very most of it. Here are a few more suggestions for you to try.

- Visit the woods at different phases of the moon and notice how it alters, how the wildlife adapts and how the changing light makes everything look slightly different.

- Forest bathing, which is simply enjoying and taking in the atmosphere of the forest and the greenery. This is good for your witchy soul.

Learn to recognize and imitate birdsong. Whistle in the woods and see which birds come closer and start singing with you. Learn to caw like a raven, hoot like an owl or coo like a wood pigeon and start a conversation with your feathered friends.

Allow wildlife to come to you. Sit or stand still, be very quiet and see who wants to make friends. It could be a stag, a raven, a fox or a squirrel. Just wait and see who introduces themselves and enjoy the interaction. Animals are naturally curious, so it will only be a matter of time before someone wants to know who you are and what you are doing in their home!

Introduce yourself to the forest. Say hello. Welcome the new buds in spring, thank the leaves as they fall to the ground in autumn. Talk to the spirits of the forest. They've been waiting for you.

Remember that no matter where you live, nature is all around you. You just have to look for it and honour it when you find it in order to live magically!

CHAPTER SIX

THE LANGUAGE AND MAGIC OF FLOWERS

Flowers are a staple of a green witch's magic. Whether she is cutting them from the garden to decorate her altar, or putting together a healing posy for a sick friend, floral tributes are a type of magic in and of themselves. Most of us have experienced the joy of being presented with an unexpected bunch of flowers, and pretty blooms are a great way to express an emotion when words might fail you. Green witches take this one step further, by adding an intention to their flower magic, giving the blooms a specific purpose. That could be that attracting love when throwing rose petals into bath water or offering strength and healing with a gift of potted lavender. Flowers can be used in many ways to enhance your green witchery. Here are a few suggestions to get you started...

- Profile flowers and herbs and their magical attributes in a special book. Simply press the plants, then fix them into a blank journal and write out the meaning and magical uses of the plant next to the pressed flowers.

- Add dried petals and blooms to homemade incense for a magical atmosphere.

- Add dried plants and flowers to spell pouches and poppets. (Poppets are hand made dolls used in spellcasting to represent the subject of the spell. They can be made of clay, wax or fabric and are popular tools in healing magic.)

- Make magical oils by placing fresh flowers, such as calendula or lavender, into a bottle and filling it with almond or sunflower oil. These bottles will make a pretty display in your witch's pantry or kitchen and you can use the oils to anoint spell candles or add to recipes for candle and soap making.

- Pressed flowers can be included in your diary, Book of Shadows or used to decorate handmade candles, soaps and baked goods.

A Victorian Posy

In the past, when personal hygiene and sanitation were poor, carrying fragrant flowers was a way to ward off unpleasant smells. Both ladies and gentlemen would frequently carry a small posy of flowers around with them. Also known as a tussie-mussie, or a nosegay, these posies could be held to the nose whenever a particularly bad smell pervaded the air, allowing the posy holder to enjoy the scent of flowers instead.

Tussie-mussies were in use from the Middle Ages, becoming more popular throughout the Tudor period, but it was Queen Victoria who made them the popular fashion accessory of the day. During her reign, the Victorian posy holder, made of fine porcelain or delicate silver, became an essential item in any affluent woman's wardrobe – and they were often presented as gifts by doting suitors or relatives.

You can make a tussie-mussie of your own by gathering fragrant herbs and flowers into a small, round posy, tying them with a ribbon and cutting the stems short. To add magic to the nosegay, choose flowers of a particular colour to draw in a specific energy, such as blue for healing, pink for self-love or red for romance. Alternatively, you can construct an entire meaning by following the guide below.

The Language of Flowers

The Victorians were keen to imbue their bouquets with "floriography", or the language of flowers, in which each bloom was thought to express a particular meaning. This effectively meant that there was something of an open secret being passed back and forth in Victorian society, via the bouquets that were being gifted. This practice is often referenced in popular literature and poetry of that time. It can be used to good effect in floral spells and rituals.

Simply use the flower – or flowers – whose meaning most closely aligns with your magical desire. The language of flowers is well documented and there are many books available that go into great detail regarding floriography if you would like to delve deeper into this topic. For now, here is a small sample of meanings for some popular flowers and plants to get you started.

- **Carnation** – Admiration, unrequited love.
- **Clover** – Industry, luck through hard work.
- **Daisy** – Innocence.
- **Dandelion** – Oracle, faithfulness, sun and moon.
- **Elder-blossom** – Compassion, wise woman skills.
- **Evergreens** – Abundance, prosperity, winter.
- **Forget-me-not** – True love, spring time.

- **Azalea** – Duty to family comes first.
- **Acacia** – Secret love.
- **Bluebell** – Constancy.
- **Bramble** – Resilience, protection, autumn.
- **Buttercup** – Childishness.

- **Foxglove** – Ambition, aspiration, insincerity.
- **Geranium** – Melancholy, recollection, reflection.
- **Gentian** – Unjust.
- **Harebell** – Submission.
- **Heather** – Solitude.
- **Henbane** – Imperfection, dangerous attraction.
- **Iris** – Message of hope.
- **Ivy** – Fidelity.
- **Jasmine** – Amiable, friendly.
- **Lavender** – Healing, answers, distrust.

- **Lilac** – First love.
- **Marigold** – Grief, sorrow.
- **Morning Glory** – Obstinacy.
- **Narcissus** – Ego, self-absorption, self-interest, self-destruction.
- **Nightshade** – Secrets, danger, vengeance.
- **Oak** – Strength, endurance, summer.
- **Orchid** – Beauty, frailty, fragility.
- **Pansy** – Thoughts, visions.
- **Poppy** – Remembrance, sleep, silence, dreams.
- **Ragwort** – Child's play, immaturity.

- **Rose** – Red – true love; Yellow – infidelity, disdain; Pink – self-love; White – rebellion.
- **Sunflower** – Haughtiness.
- **Sweet William (Stinking Billy)** – Treachery, betrayal, battle.
- **Thistle** – Defiance, defence, retaliation, retribution.
- **Tulip** – "Do you like me too?" An invitation to an affair (especially when mixed with yellow roses!)
- **Violet** – Modesty, steadfastness, shyness.
- **Water Lily** – Pure-hearted.

- **Willow** – Pretentiousness, downfall, "reap as you've sown".
- **Yarrow** – A declaration of war, conflict (especially when mixed with Sweet William).
- **Yew** – Death, rebirth, ancestors.

Floromancy

Floromancy is the art of divination or fortune-telling, using flowers, leaves and petals. Many people have plucked the petals from a daisy to determine if someone loves them or not, but there are lots of other ways to use flowers for fortune-telling purposes. Here are just a few:

- Take two potted marigold flowers and place them on a sunny window sill. Label one pot "Yes" and the other "No". Stand before them and ask a question that requires a simple yes/no reply. Keep an eye on the flowers and, as the sun sets, see which flower closes first and note which pot it's in to find your answer.

- As blossom or leaves start to fall from trees, pick out a single leaf or petal and make a wish. If you finish making your wish before the petal lands on the ground it will come true, if not it won't.

- Whenever you see the first flower of spring, it will determine your fortune for the rest of the year. To see it on a Monday means good luck, Tuesday means success, Wednesday means a marriage within the year, Thursday means you should be careful and cautious, Friday means prosperity, Saturday means misfortune will dog your heels and Sunday means great opportunities and lucky chances.

- Tradition states that the first letter of the first flower you find in spring will also be the first initial of a new love interest.

- Having an odd number of cut flowers in a vase is considered lucky.

- Floral superstitions also denote that having white lilies in the home is bad luck as they are associated with funerals.

- Lilac should never be cut for indoors or this will anger the fey folk.

- A mix of red and white flowers is also considered bad luck as in some cultures these are the colours of funeral wreaths.

- Wearing or growing the flower of your birth month is thought to bring good luck to you.

January – Carnation
February – Violet
March – Daffodil
April – Daisy
May – Lily of the Valley
June – Rose
July – Cornflower

August – Poppy
September – Gladioli
October – Marigold
November – Chrysanthemum
December – Holly

How to Make a Midsummer Flower Crown

Items required: Florist wire, wire cutters, ribbon, flowers of your choice.
Timing: Make on Midsummer's Day.

It is traditional in pagan circles to make and wear a flower crown on Midsummer's Day. They are easy enough to make – all you need to do is wrap florist wire around your head two or three times to make a crown of the correct size. Twist the end of the wire around the crown to secure it, then begin to weave your chosen flowers into the circlet, securing with additional florist wire if necessary. You can use bright gold and orange flowers to represent the sun at its strongest, or you can choose flower colours that match your intention: blue for healing, pink for self-love, white for new beginnings, green for abundance and so on. Once you have placed all your flowers around the crown, add ribbon to decorate and to cover any sharp stems, tying the ends into a pretty bow at the back of the crown. Then wear the crown as part of your Midsummer solstice celebrations.

Essential Oils

If you don't have access to fresh flowers, then essential oils are your new best friends! Not only do they hold all the same magical attributes as fresh flowers, they take up less space and can be used all year round, so you don't need to wait for them to come into season. Most witches have a collection of essential oils because they are so useful.

In magic, essential oils are used to anoint spell candles, poppets and pouches. They can be simmered to fragrance a space, or added to water to create room sprays or eco-friendly cleaning products. In addition, they can be used when making your own candles, soaps, lotions and potions, plus they have the added benefit of making good massage blends for aromatherapy.

There are lots of different essential oils for you to choose from, but some of the most useful are lavender, tea tree, ylang-ylang, eucalyptus, peppermint, bergamot, rose, geranium, patchouli, clary sage and chamomile. Keep your oils in a dark place – maybe in a wooden box or a cupboard – and remember that a little goes a long way. Bear in mind that most oils, with the exception of lavender and tea tree, need to be diluted in a carrier, such as almond oil, before they're applied to the skin. Essential oils are a vital part of any witch's kit, so treat yourself to one or two and start to experiment with them in your spellcraft.

CHAPTER SEVEN
THE POISON PATHWAY

Not all plants are beneficial. Some are dangerous, even lethal, to both humans and animals. In the wrong hands, such plants can be weaponized as poisons, which is what Catherine de Medici had a reputation for doing – using witch's plants to poison her rivals and political opponents. To this day, poison is still commonly thought of as a woman's weapon of choice for murder, though this is disputed among criminologists and could simply be a lingering form of misogyny.

Many toxic plants grow wild in woodlands and hedgerows – some might even be growing in your own garden without your knowledge. We might not like to admit it, but it cannot be denied that some of the most toxic and dangerous plants have long been associated with witches and witchcraft, so it is wise to know what they are so that you can avoid them and practise safely.

The Poison Garden

A beautifully landscaped garden with a deadly difference, the Poison Garden in the English county of Northumberland has a foreboding appearance. Part of Alnwick Garden, adjacent to the town's castle, the small but deadly space is kept safely locked away behind tall, black iron gates bearing the symbol of the skull and crossbones to denote the lethal powers of the plants within.

You can only see the Poison Garden by guided tour, as it would be too dangerous to allow people to wander around freely. Deceptively, it looks so pretty – and many of the poisonous plants growing there are quite common, including foxgloves and laurel. It just goes to show that common garden plants can have a darker side that we might not be aware of, so it pays to be mindful and to do your research thoroughly when dealing with plants.

Witch's Herbs

Several plants always make people think of witches and witchcraft. Known as "witch's herbs", hemlock, belladonna, henbane and mandrake are all closely associated with the magical arts – and all of them are lethal! Of course, no plant is the sole agent of its toxicity; it needs human intervention to administer it – whether this be via an accidental berry-picking excursion or a pre-meditated homicide, these plants need human hands to cause harm and death.

That said, only a fool would underestimate the power of such plants, so if you plan to grow them or pick them from the wilderness, always wear surgical gloves and wash your hands thoroughly afterwards, as ingesting even a small amount can have a very harmful effect. Also be aware, while it isn't illegal to grow poisonous plants in your garden, you should not allow them to spread into your neighbours' gardens or grass verges. You will also be held responsible should any children or pets ingest them and be harmed as a result. As most of these plants grow in the wild anyway, it might be safest to admire them from afar and let the Forestry Commission look after them!

Belladonna

Atropa belladonna, or deadly nightshade as it is more commonly known, is widespread throughout the UK, Europe and in certain areas of the US. All parts of deadly nightshade are lethal, from root to flower tip, and ingesting just a small number of berries is enough to kill a child. This plant prefers damp soil and thrives in woodlands, meadows and riverside spots, so those are the areas where you are likely to find it growing wild. It can be identified by its purple, bell-like flowers and extremely shiny black berries.

Due to the hallucinogenic properties of belladonna, it is one of the plants that is associated with witches' "flying ointment", which was a concoction of psychoactive plants reduced to an ointment administered to cause the sensation of flying. However, belladonna is so toxic that just touching it without gloves can cause painful blisters, so one wonders what the side effects to such a flying ointment might have been!

In mythology, deadly nightshade is linked to the Crone aspect of the goddess and in particular to Atropos, the oldest of the Three Fates in Greek mythology, and Skuld of the Norns (the Scandinavian equivalent), who both sever the thread of life. It is a plant that is inherently associated with death and its potential to cause it. Belladonna's witchy history is celebrated on the night of Walpurgis, April 30, also known as Witches' Night or May Eve.

Henbane

Another member of the nightshade family is *Hyoscyamus niger*, or henbane, also known as "stinking nightshade," due to its pungent, somewhat fishy smell. It grows wild in waterlogged places such as riversides, dykes and ditches and can be identified by the creamy yellow trumpet flowers that are black at the centre. Like its cousin, belladonna, all parts of henbane are poisonous and lethal if ingested. Again, it is thought to have been used as part of "flying ointment" because of its power to induce visions and delirium, although too much could lead to madness and death, so I don't recommend trying to recreate this ointment! Historically, henbane was used to tip poison arrows by the Gauls and Greeks, while the Druids and Vikings used the plant in death rituals and funeral rites. In Greek mythology, henbane was added to the potions made by the enchantress Medea.

Hemlock

Conium maculatum, or hemlock, is associated with funeral rites, particularly in Germanic regions. It thrives in watery ground along rivers and can spring up just about anywhere that is left undisturbed. It is a hardy plant, commonly known as "poison parsley", because its leaves resemble the harmless culinary herb and mistakes can prove fatal. Hemlock can be identified by its pretty white flowers in spring and summer, while its stems have purplish-red spots on them. In Christian mythology, these spots were said to have been the blood of Jesus as hemlock grew on the site of his crucifixion. As a result, it was cursed to be a fatally poisonous plant. Touching hemlock without gloves can cause bouts of dizziness and vertigo, and the plant can cause impotence in men. Ingestion can lead to convulsions, hallucinations, delirium, coma and slow death, so it is not a plant to meddle with. In ancient Greece, hemlock was the weapon of choice for state executions and it was famously responsible for the death of the philosopher Socrates.

Wolfsbane

Aconitum or wolfsbane, also known as monkshood, is a plant with lovely purple or yellow flowers that resemble the hood of a monk's habit. It is often found in herbaceous borders as many people are not aware of its high level of toxicity and it is attractive to bees and butterflies. Sometimes referred to as "the queen of poisons", all parts of wolfsbane are poisonous. In the past it was used to kill wolves, particularly in agricultural areas, hence the name. Again, the juice of this plant has been used to tip poison arrows and it has been said to both cure and cause lycanthropy. In popular folklore, lycanthropy was the belief that some people could turn into werewolves during the time of the full moon. This condition was thought to be brought about by being bitten by a wolf or werewolf, leading to the condition of lycanthropy and the werewolf legends.

Wormwood

This is the plant of the green fairy. *Artemisia absinthium* – or wormwood – is the key ingredient in absinthe. *Le fee vert*, or the green fairy, is said to be the spirit of the wormwood plant and can be communed with by drinking absinthe. This fairy was thought to offer the gift of inspiration, hence the popularity of absinthe among artists, poets and writers during the Romantic period. The plant's botanical name links it with the goddess Artemis, who is associated with the hunt and therefore the woods and foliage. Wormwood was used as an antiseptic and to treat intestinal worms.

Mandrake

Mandragora officinarum, or mandrake, is famously associated with witchcraft. Both the roots and leaves are highly toxic. However, the humanoid shape of the root meant that it was perfect to use as a poppet in spell casting. A member of the nightshade family, mandrake has similar hypnotic and hallucinogenic properties to belladonna and henbane. In the past it was used as a sedative and tranquilizer. Carrying a mandrake root was also said to bring good fortune, though to pull one up by the roots and hear its scream would cause instant death, so presumably you would have to get someone *else* to harvest this particular good-luck charm on your behalf! Sometimes byrony roots would be used as a magical substitute if mandragora wasn't available. In folklore, mandrake was said to thrive in the bloody soil of execution sites, gallows and battle fields.

Fly Agaric Fairy Rings

Amanita muscaria is the red fly agaric mushroom with white spots, which is synonymous with magic and fairy enchantment. It is a native fungus of the UK and they grow in woodlands from late summer to autumn. Historically they were used as pesticides to kill flies. They are highly poisonous and psychoactive, causing hallucinations, vomiting, seizures and delirium. They are probably the prettiest and most easily recognisable of all mushrooms, owing in part to their appearance in children's books and fairy tales, where they are usually depicted as being fairy homes and thrones.

In folklore, a ring of fly agaric mushrooms, also known as a "fairy ring", is said to be a portal into the land of the fey folk. If you find such a ring then you have been invited to dance with the fairies, but if you eat or drink anything while in the fairy realm, you will never be able to return to your own world. The toxic properties of fly agaric mushrooms were also used in witch's flying ointment and could account for the tales of fairy revels that are associated with this magical toadstool.

So, there you have it – some the most poisonous plants associated with witchcraft. It should go without saying that this chapter is for information only and I don't recommend that you experiment with any of these plants. But it is always useful to be able to identify them, especially when you are out in woods foraging, because mistakes can be lethal. Take care and use your common sense.

CHAPTER EIGHT

GREEN WITCH ENVIRONMENTALISM

Working closely with the natural world, green witches are obviously keen to protect the environment. Regarding the Earth as our mother means that we have a deep connection with the green spaces around us, whether we live in the countryside or in large cities. While the term eco-warrior is somewhat dated, many green witches are active in areas such as conservation, rewilding and protection of natural spaces that are under threat from capitalism and a surging population. It can be a difficult path to walk: while everyone deserves a roof over their heads, the clearance of forests and natural areas for development takes something away from all of us. Progress should not have to come at the expense of the environment.

Caring for the planet doesn't have to involve protest marches or living in condemned trees for weeks on end, although that can be part of your strategy if you want it to be. It can also mean gentler ways of caring for the Earth by changing the way you live day to day, trying to take responsibility for your own personal impact on the world and your contribution to issues such as global warming, the negative impact of plastic, consumerism and the landfill that goes with it, and so on. Such steps might not be enough to change the habits of the world at large, but every change you want to see in society needs to begin with you, so here are a few suggestions as to how you can start to live a greener life that is more attuned with Mother Nature.

How to Live a Greener Life

Living a greener life is all about making small changes to your daily routine until they become your new habits. Green or slow living can be a welcome escape from the frenetic world in which we live. By simply slowing down your life and being more mindful of the things you do and how they impact the world around you, you will begin to feel more in tune with nature, rather than separate from it. Here are a few ideas for you try out to get started with a greener way of living.

- Walk as much as possible. Walk to work if you can, or walk the kids to school, instead of driving. See this as a time to breathe in the fresh air and to notice the world around you, the changes in the trees, the birds building nests, and so on. You miss all this when driving a car.

- If you can't walk to work, cycle there instead. Or use public transport and do some discreet people-watching. Who are your fellow passengers? Try to imagine what kind of lives they lead and how their day differs from yours.

- Borrow, don't buy. This one is a great change to make for all those things that you would normally buy without a second thought. If you love reading, use the local libraries in your area, or see if you can swap your old books for used ones in a second-hand bookstore. Borrow clothes from friends and family, or start a "swap group" with people who have similar interests and needs. For instance, you could get a group of mothers together and swap maternity clothes, or baby items.

🌀 Recycle and repurpose old items to give them a new lease of life. Sometimes all something needs is a coat of paint and a bit of imagination. If you are artistic, try painting flowers, animals and woodland scenes, representing your "witchcore" vibes, on an old piece of furniture to make it stand out from the crowd.

🌀 Donate as much as you can. We all have things we no longer use or need, so instead of throwing them away, donate them to a charity shop, a shelter or somewhere similar. Sadly, these days there are food, baby, pet and clothing banks springing up all over the place, so donating your unwanted items there will ensure they go to people who need them most.

🌀 Go foraging for mushrooms (make sure you have a guide to ensure you don't pick a poisonous one), nuts and berries, instead of buying them at the supermarket.

🌀 Grow your own produce if you can. You don't need a huge space for a small crop of tomatoes or strawberries or to grow herbs for spellcraft and cooking.

- Let the grass grow! Allow part of your garden to rewild, or plant wildflowers. This will encourage bees and other pollinating insects. Pretty flowers will attract pretty butterflies so it's a win-win situation.

- Try to eat less meat and dairy, or adopt a vegan diet if that appeals.

- Avoid using plastic, so take your own bags to the supermarket, use a reusable drinking bottle or cup and invest in reusable straws.

- Have a "Witch Swap" with like-minded friends and swap crystals, card decks and magical tools. Just remember to ritually cleanse your new treasures before you use them.

Casting Spells for the Environment

As well as trying to reduce their own negative impact on the environment, green witches also like to cast spells to protect it. This type of magic takes many forms, from invoking guardian spirits to watch over threatened trees and green spaces, to casting for the ethical and humane treatment of livestock.

It makes sense that a witch would use magic to address these issues, because she is, in effect, using her own spiritual power to heal and protect the greater power of the Earth, which she connects with in her magic. This kind of symbiosis carries with it the responsibility to act as a guardian of the Earth when necessary. This could be something as simple as a dispute with a neighbour who wants you to cut down trees growing in your garden because *he* doesn't like them, in which case you would need to defend their right to grow. Or it could be more complex, in the form of a co-ordinated spell with other witches to protect an area from development. Witchcraft is the art of transformation by spellwork, so making magic to transform the damage done to the Earth is the responsibility of every witch.

Blessing of Sacrifice

Farming animals for the food industry is a fact of life all over the world. Whether you are vegetarian, vegan, or neither, these animals should be honoured for their sacrifice – even if you do not eat meat yourself – and they should be defended and protected against cruel or inhumane treatment, including during their slaughter.

The full moon of October is known as the Blood Moon, because this was traditionally the time when livestock would be slaughtered and salted in order to provide meat for the coming winter months. This was a kind of ritual slaughter, where the animals were honoured for their sacrifice. In modern farming, animals are routinely sent to the slaughterhouse and meat is readily available throughout the year for those who choose to eat it. It is a great shame that their sacrifice goes largely unnoticed and is taken for granted. One thing green witches can do is honour the spirits of slaughtered livestock, as not only does this mark their sacrifice, it also connects us to our pagan ancestors. This spell is designed to bless and honour the livestock that is destined for the food industry.

Blessing for Livestock

Items required: One black candle, one red candle, red thread, a plate to hold them.

Moon phase: Cast on the Blood or Full Moon in October or on Samhain (October 31 – November 1).

You will need two candles, one black and one red. Tie them together with a piece of red thread and stand them on a plate, using a little melted wax from the bottom of the candles to secure them in place. Hold your hands over the candles and say:

> I honour the passing of all slaughtered beasts
>
> Who give their lives so that we might feast
>
> With honour and reverence, respect and love
>
> I give thanks to the creatures of Earth and the powers above.
>
> Blessed be and thank you for your sacrifice.

Light both the candles and leave them in place until they have burned out naturally. Give extra thanks for any meat-based dishes that make up your diet.

Share the Love Spell

Items required: An apple, athame (ceremonial blade) or knife, pentacle, water.
Moon phase: Perform during a waxing moon.

This is a great little spell to give your love to the Earth Mother by sharing an apple, the fruit of love, with her. Take an apple out to a natural spot, such as your garden or a woodland. Cut it in half across the equator line to expose the five-pointed star of seeds at the centre. Scoop out the seeds and place them on the pentacle as you eat one half of the apple. Then say:

This fruit of love I give to the Earth

That she may give these seeds rebirth

Apples green and apples red

Come into bloom from your earthly bed.

Plant the apple seeds into the soil and water them, then leave the other half of the apple as a final offering for any wild creature that wishes to enjoy it.

Spell to Protect a Tree

Items required: Lavender oil, a small cat's bell, red thread.
Moon phase: Full moon.

If you know of any tree that is under threat of being cut down, cast this spell to help protect it. On the night of the full moon, go out to the tree, taking with you a small cat's bell hung on a length of red thread and a bottle of lavender essential oil. Place your hands on the trunk of the tree and send your loving strength into the bark. Visualize a green light passing from your palms into the trunk and lighting up the tree from the inside. Next hang the bell from one of the branches with the red thread and, as you do so, say:

> Ring out danger, ring out harm
> Ring out loud and sound the alarm
> When woodsmen come to chop and fell
> Their work is thwarted by this spell
> Long life to this tree, protected be
> Long life to this tree, so shall it be!

As a final step, draw the Algiz protection rune onto the tree trunk, using the lavender oil, then bless the tree and know that you have done what you can to cast a spell of protection around it. Whatever the outcome, the spirit of the tree will know that you tried to help.

Invoke a Land Deva

Items required: A stone or crystal.
Moon phase: Full moon.

If you know that an area is under threat from developers or vandals, then invoking a land deva is a good way to keep such intruders away. Land devas are spirits of the Earth and guardians of the green. Their presence can be enough to scare away those who come to the area with bad intentions. To invoke a land deva to protect a tree or a green space, go there and sit on the ground. Close your eyes and visualize the deva of the land rising up from the ground in front of you and say:

> Spirit of Earth, I invoke you to protect this sacred space
>
> Let none come here with ill intent, but make them flee before you
>
> Help us to keep this area green and growing, its life energies free and flowing
>
> Wild and untamed, free and unfettered, send intruders away until they learn better
>
> May your presence and the magic imbued in this stone keep this place green and whole
>
> So mote it be.

Leave the stone or crystal in a hidden place within the area that you are trying to protect.

> I speak out my truth with a cheer!

CHAPTER NINE

GREEN WITCH ACTIVISM AND EMPOWERMENT

Green witches are often involved in activism, as well as environmentalism. While they cast spells for the protection of the natural world, activist witches also cast for the improvement of society, both at home and abroad. This could mean working spells for the demise of terrorist organisations, or rituals to uphold the rights of women. In this respect, witchcraft meets politics, and many a green witch has penned her signature on petitions for the abolition of fox hunting, the right to abortion, sanctuary for asylum seekers and so on.

While, on the surface, it might seem as if political issues have little or nothing to do with witchcraft, in fact nothing could be further from the truth. We all have to live in the society that we create, both locally and globally. The internet has also had a big impact, because it has made us more aware of what is going on in other parts of the world, and the tensions and conflicts that people are having to endure. Witchery is a good way to send out positive energy to the places that need it most. It can be as simple as lighting a candle and sending love to the world.

Modern Witch Hunts

Although witches are free to practise their craft safely in some parts of the world, in others, witch hunts are still going on. We might like to believe that witch hunting has been consigned to the history books, but in Sub-Saharan Africa, Brazil and India people are still being accused of witchcraft. Just as with the witch craze of the past, the majority of those accused in today's witch hunts tend to be elderly women or, sometimes, children – people who are vulnerable and therefore easy targets.

In some countries, witch trials are actually taking place in courts, or in village tribunals that have been set up for that specific purpose. It seems unbelievable that such trials have any place in the modern world, but sadly they still exist. Lynching is not uncommon, along with beatings and torture. Accused witches are frequently forced to drink toxic potions that are thought to rid them of evil spirits, but which often kill them. In some parts of the world, just owning an amulet or good luck charm is enough to get you killed for being a witch. Green witches can help by raising awareness of this issue on social media platforms and, of course, we can also cast spells.

Spell to Let the Hunters Become the Hunted

Items required: An image of Artemis, a tealight candle and holder.
Moon phase: Full moon.

In Greek mythology, Artemis is the goddess of the hunt, who caught the huntsman Actaeon watching her bathe. As punishment, she turned him into a stag and he was killed by his own hounds. In this spell, we call on Artemis to help us to turn the tide against the modern-day witch hunters. Take the image of Artemis and, in front of it, place the tealight in the holder. Light the candle and concentrate on the image of the goddess. Imagine her retribution being paid out to the witch hunters as you say the incantation below three times.

Let the hunters be hunted, let the victims run free

Let the witches be valiant while their
persecutors flee

Let the arrows of Artemis strike at their hearts

As the foe of all witches, the witch hunter departs!

So mote it be.

#MeToo and #BlackLivesMatter

In recent years we have seen a surge of public empowerment with marches and protests at the systemic sexism, misogyny and racism that pervade society. Such movements have led to more awareness of these underlying issues. People are having to reassess how they behave and to adjust how they interact with others and become more inclusive.

Large organisations, such as the Ministry of Defence, the BBC, the police service and even Parliament itself, are finally beginning to understand that they cannot simply brush sexual harassment or racism under the rug as they might have done before. The public will no longer stand for it and these organisations are now held accountable for the actions of the people who work for them.

Abuse of any kind should never be tolerated in society and when someone in a position of power uses it to abuse others, then that is a serious transgression that must be tackled and brought to light, regardless of whether that person is an MP or a pilot, a police officer, a soldier or a celebrity. Fame, fortune and diplomatic immunity should offer them no protection when they abuse their position.

Furthermore, it can be incredibly damaging for a victim to watch their abuser win promotions, accolades and celebrity status, when their own life lies in tatters around them, because someone abused their position. Sadly, we have seen what the consequences are when such behaviour goes unchallenged. The spell below is designed to keep the bad apples in check. Use it in conjunction with the Artemis spell above for the best results.

Spell for Binding Those Who Abuse Their Power

Items required: An apple, athame or knife, garlic powder.
Moon phase: Waning moon.

Using the athame, carve the name of the abuser into the apple skin, along with the organisation they are connected to. Sprinkle the apple with garlic powder to banish their behaviour, then bury the apple deep in the earth as you say:

Misunderstandings are no excuse

I shine a light on your abuse

Misdemeanours you've hidden well

But I have a voice, I'll show and tell!

I'll blow the whistle to end your game

Let the truth be known, you're named and shamed.

Diversity and Tolerance

There is no doubt that society is changing and at a rapid pace. It can be hard to keep up and even harder to stay on the right side of what is currently viewed as being politically correct. Social interactions can be a minefield and an innocent remark can quickly blow up in your face to become so much more. This is especially true for those of us who are quite outspoken! It can seem as if everyone is looking for an opportunity to be offended and, while people have the right to be offended by something you say, they do *not* have the right to choose your words for you! Of course, I am not suggesting that you go out of your way to be mean, spiteful or deliberately offensive. What I *am* saying is that society is made up of so many different cultures and points of view that it is perhaps inevitable that people will clash at some point.

Diversity is one of the great strengths of modern society. Think how boring the world would be if we were all exactly the same. That said, it can, at times, be quite difficult to empathize with someone who is on a completely different path from you. But, here's the thing – you don't have to *understand* everyone's perspective in depth. You don't have to understand all the complex mental and emotional needs that set someone on the transgender or non-binary path, for instance. You just have to step back and let them get on with it, so that they feel free and safe to live the life of *their* choice. That's it. That's all you have to do – live and let live, with harm to none.

Live and Let Live Spell

Items required: A piece of paper and a pen, a cauldron or heatproof dish, lighter.
Moon phase: Full moon.

This simple spell calls for a more tolerant society, as well as being a reminder to yourself to be more tolerant and understanding towards people who are living a different kind of life. You do not know what struggles anyone else is enduring, so be kind to others and cast this spell for wider tolerance in your community. Write the following incantation on a piece of paper, chant it three times, then burn the paper in the cauldron to release the spell.

All colours, all creeds, all loves be as one

All nations, all notions of self-redone

All styles, all images, viewed as an art

All spirits and religions that come
from the heart

Live and let live in love and in trust

Live and let live, tolerance is a must.

Refuse To Be Silenced!

While we should be kind to those who are on a different path to us, it is also important not to allow yourself to be silenced, simply for fear of causing offence. You have every right to form and present your own opinions, providing you do so respectfully. However, these days it can feel like we are in danger of being shouted down whenever we voice an unpopular opinion. This is dangerous, because silencing people is usually the first step in any dictatorship. Freedom to speak your mind and to have a free press that holds governments accountable for their actions are vital parts of any democratic society. Without free speech, we are a mute nation of bystanders. With free speech, we are a nation of activists and protestors – and a force to be reckoned with!

Speak Your Truth Spell

Items required: A white candle and holder, a lighter
Moon phase: New moon.

Cast this spell whenever you feel the need to get something off your chest, or to speak up for others in society. It's a good one to cast the night before attending any protest march too. Light the white candle and focus on the flame as you imagine getting your point across, peacefully, but with conviction. Visualize the changes that might come to pass if your opinions are taken seriously and your suggestions acted upon. When you can see this clearly in your mind, repeat the following chant three times, then let the candle burn down naturally.

Blessed be those who are different

Blessed be those who are the same

Blessed be my voice raised in protest

Blessed be those who are blamed

In love and in trust I break silence

In valour and strength, I face fear

In peaceful, harmonious cadence

CHAPTER TEN

GREEN LIVING AND GIVING

Giving back to the planet is all part of the green witch life, so along with spells for environmental and activism issues, witches often work locally to give a bit of their energy back to the green spaces around them. In this final chapter, we are going to look at simple ways you can give back to Mother Nature who nurtures all of us so well.

Adopt a Tree

Taking a special interest in a tree in your local area is one way to reconnect with the nature of your environment. See this as a kind of voluntary adoption and begin to spend time near the tree, learning about it and bringing offerings to place at its roots. Saplings are great for children to adopt because they grow so quickly, like young humans do. Older trees can make wise companions and are great for meditating beneath, or just sitting near and contemplating. Feed the roots with libations of cider or ale, perhaps sharing a tipple each evening as you walk the dog. Trace runes of protection on the bark and hang food for the birds from its branches. Eventually you will feel that you have made a true friend in the tree and your symbiotic relationship will begin to thrive.

Litterbug Buster

Taking part in a litter-picking session – or organising one with your friends – is another way green witches can give back. You can do this as a solitary practice, taking a bin bag and picking up the litter in an untidy part of your local community. Spending an hour pulling empty crisps packets and sweet wrappers from the hedgerows – perhaps as you walk back from dropping the kids off at school – is a good way to show environmental awareness and to teach your children to be more aware too. For larger, organized litter-picking excursions, you may need permission from your local council, which can also provide you with some useful equipment to help the job along. Make sure to keep a first aid kit with you, in case of accidents from broken glass or tin cans.

Create a Community Garden

If there is a small area of wasteland near your home, seek permission from the council to turn it into a community garden, where you can plant flowers and herbs. Tend the garden well, so that the council can see this is an asset to the area and gather friends and neighbours to help you weed and plant. In this way, you are creating a pretty green space that everyone can enjoy. As an alternative, you could use an allotment to grow vegetables and then donate them to food banks or soup kitchens.

A Forest Witch Tea Party

Items required: A picnic basket and blanket, your favourite sandwiches, cakes, nuts, seeds, apples, peanut butter, juice to drink, a few large pine cones, florist wire or thread, athame or knife.

Moon phase: A summery day during a waxing moon is best.

Is there anything more enchanting than enjoying a picnic in the woods? It feels like the kind of thing the witches of old would have done, and whether you go alone or with friends, there is something very spiritual about taking food out into the forest and inviting your woodland friends to partake with you. For this ritual, you are going to pack a basket with all good things to eat, but your picnic will be one with a difference – you are going to be making food for the birds, squirrels and deer to enjoy, as well as you and your friends.

To begin, wrap florist wire around each pine cone, leaving enough wire at the top to hang it. Then fill the pine cones with peanut butter, spreading it quite thickly. Next roll the buttered pine cone through a mixture of seeds suitable for wild birds. Put the cones into a lunchbox and keep them in the fridge overnight.

On the day of the forest tea party, make your favourite sandwiches and fill your picnic basket with sweet cakes and something to drink. Next add a bag of mixed nuts suitable for wildlife, the buttered pine cones from the fridge, apples, a jar of runny honey, a saucer and the athame. Throw a picnic blanket and a good book on top and you are ready to go out into the woods. Once there, spread out your blanket and invite your woodland friends to tea with the following incantation.

Friends of fur, friends of air,

I offer up these gifts to share

A picnic here I place this day

Feel free to come and join the fray

Nuts and fruits and seeds and treats

Come join with me, as good things we eat!

All are welcome!

Blessed be.

Hang the pine cones from the nearby trees, place piles of nuts and apple slices on the forest floor at a slight distance so that the wildlife feel safe to enjoy them. Finally, for your insect friends, pour some honey onto the saucer and place this on the forest floor too, safely away from your own picnic area. Then sit down, eat your picnic, read your book and enjoy spending time with the wildlife. You can leave the nuts and fruit in the forest when you leave, but be sure to take the saucer and all your litter away with you. *Bon appétit!*

AFTERWORD

Step into The Living Light

The path of the green witch is filled with living light. It sparkles in the dewdrops on cobwebs, in the sunshine on dancing leaves and in the glimmer of moss, stretching out like a shimmering green carpet before you. It welcomes you into the forest with the heraldic call of a crow, the squirrels guiding your steps as they leap from branch to branch and tree to tree, escorting you along the mystic trail. It beckons from the brook and sings through the trees, as the bluebells bow their heads in reverence when you pass by. It is an enchanting practice, one that brings you closer to nature and the world at large.

I hope that you have enjoyed our little foray into the enchanted forest together and that you have found information and practices in this book to both inspire and empower you. While green witchery can be hard work at times, particularly in the garden, and it carries a certain weight of environmental responsibility, it is a very life-affirming practice that honours the Earth Mother and the Green Man. It is certainly the magical path for the fey-hearted, so let your roots dig deep and your boughs stretch high, as you become the forest-green witch you were meant to be! Farewell my fey-hearted friend, until our next merry meeting.

Serene blessings,

Marie Bruce x